C000059697

Other 'crazy' gigglebooks by Bill Stott
Cats – they drive us crazy!
Marriage – it drives us crazy!
Football – it drives us crazy!
Rugby – it drives us crazy!

Published simultaneously in 2004 by Exley Publications Ltd in Great
Britain, and Exley Publications LLC in the USA

12 11 10 9 8 7 6 5 4 3 2

Selection and arrangement copyright © 2004 Helen Exley
Cartoons copyright © 2004 Bill Stott
Design by <rog@monkeyboydesign.co.uk>

ISBN 1-86187-756-0

A copy of the CIP data is available from the British Library on request.
All rights reserved. No part of this publication may be reproduced or
transmitted in any form or by any means without permission in writing
from the publisher.

Printed in China

Helen Exley Giftbooks, 16 Chalk Hill, Watford, Herts, WD19 4BG, UK
Helen Exley Giftbooks, 185 Main Street, Spencer MA 01562, USA
www.helenexleygiftbooks.com

A HELEN EXLEY GIGGLEBOOK

Sex

IT DRIVES US CRAZY!

CARTOONS BY BILL STOTT

"Oh all right...
 but only during the breaks."

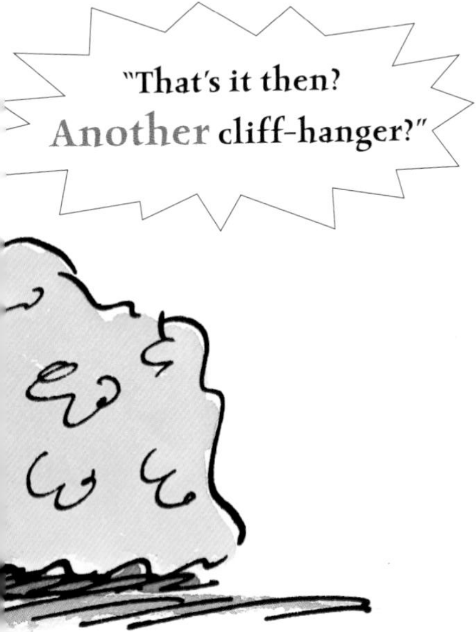
"That's it then? Another cliff-hanger?"

You're right.
That is impossible.
The book's upside down."

"You'd better put the year on, otherwise people will think we do it every day."

"Sorry Dear – did you say something? I must have dozed off..."

"My mother would absolutely
kill me if she could see me now!"

"Yes, very nice but when I said why don't we dress up, that's not quite what I meant."

"That looks like a hairpiece too!"

"Why don't I turn the light out then you can stop holding your breath and let your tummy out?"

"STOP! STOP!
One of my lenses is missing!"

"My mother's told me about boys like you – but I never thought I'd find one!"

"Gerald?
It's time!"

"To be honest, I'd rather you faked it instead of finishing your book half-way through!"

"NO! NO! It's my heart –
don't let them out!"

"Helping you on with your socks after the main event does rather take the edge off it!"

"Get in quickly, you
    clash with the new quilt."

"Couldn't you just lie when I ask what you're thinking, instead of saying 'I wonder who won the golf'?"

"I seem to remember you saying our foreplay was becoming rather predictable... well..."

"Other women just get headaches..."

"Perhaps you'd like a bit of a rest?"

"I've just had a fantastic
idea for your thesis!
And, we could do all the
experiments right here!"

"No the earth hasn't moved...
I've got cramp."

"I bet Brad Pitt never takes his boxers off before his shirt..."

"Don't sulk. You asked me what I wanted and I told you – an egg, sunny side up."

SAMANTHA
THE
INFLATABLE
COMPANION
SLIGHTLY
IMPERFECT

"Ingook, I've got the hots
for you... er... that is Ingook?"

"And in the very near future I see you needing dental treatment unless you take your hand off my knee..."

"Do go on Mrs Spotwick – you were telling me your husband has no sense of time or place..."

"This yours?"

"See? I knew you could manage it without your medallions!"

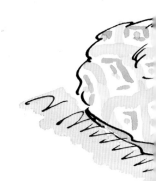

About Bill Stott

Bill Stott is a freelance cartoonist whose work never fails to pinpoint the absurd and simply daft moments in our daily lives. Originally Head of Arts faculty at a city high school, Bi launched himself as a freelance cartoonist in 1976. With sales of 2.8 million books with Helen Exley Giftbooks, Bill has an impressive portfolio of 26 published titles, including his very successful *Spread of Over 40's Jokes* and *Triumph of Over 50's Jokes*.

Bill's work appears in many publications and magazines, ranging from the *The Times Educational Supplement* to *Practical Poultry*. An acclaimed after-dinner speaker, Bill subjects his audience to a generous helping of his wit and wisdom, illustrated with cartoons drawn deftly on the spot!

What is a Helen Exley giftbook?

We hope you enjoy *Sex – it drives us crazy!*. It's just one of many hilarious cartoon books available from Helen Exley Giftbooks, all of which make special gifts. We try our best to bring you the funniest jokes because we want every book we publish to be great to give, great to receive.

HELEN EXLEY GIFTBOOKS creates gifts for all special occasions – not just birthdays, anniversaries, weddings and Christmas, but for those times when you just want to say 'thanks' or 'I love you'. Why not visit our website, www. helenexleygiftbooks.com, and browse through all our present ideas?

ALSO BY BILL STOTT
Cats – they drive us crazy!
Football – it drives us crazy!
Rugby – it drives us crazy!
Marriage – it drives us crazy!

Information on all our titles is also available from
Helen Exley Giftbooks, 16 Chalk Hill, Watford WD19 4BG, UK. Tel 01923 250505
Helen Exley Giftbooks, 185 Main Street, Spencer MA 01562, USA. Tel 877 395 3942